STAY

Also by Kathleen McGookey

Whatever Shines
(Marie Alexander Poetry Series)

We'll See: Poems by Georges L. Godeau (translation)

October Again (chapbook)

Mended (chapbook)

Stay

prose poems

Kathleen McGookey

Press 53
Winston-Salem

Press 53, LLC
PO Box 30314
Winston-Salem, NC 27130

First Edition

A Tom Lombardo Poetry Selection

Cover design by Kevin Morgan Watson

Cover art, "The World Spins," Copyright © 2012
by Dawn D. Surratt, used by permission of the artist.

Author photo by Kaitlin LaMoine Martin

Printed on acid-free paper
ISBN 978-1-941209-28-8

In memory of my parents,
for my brother,
and, as always, for Rhys

The worst thing you can imagine
is not the worst thing that can happen to you.

–Gary Young

Acknowledgments

The author wishes to gratefully acknowledge the editors and staff of the periodicals where the following poems originally appeared, sometimes in different versions.

basalt, "Another Ache"
Chariton Review, "Joy"
Chelsea, "The Accident" and "Notes on the Accident"
Cloudbank, "Seaside Lullaby for My Friend"
Court Green, "Flight," "Lament at Bath Time" and "Morning"
Epoch, "Onion"
Eclipse, "Everlasting," "Grief's Pretty Prize" and "Sorrow Came"
Ellipsis, "Punishment" (as "I'd like my pain removed....")
Faultline, "Near the Angel"
Great River Review, "Cure"
Hanging Loose, "Siege"
Hotel Amerika, "Shallow"
Hubbub, "Lament"
The Journal, "Details"
Lumberyard, "Fallen"
Mid-American Review, "No Comfort"
MiPoesias, "My Anger at Home"
New Ohio Review, "After," "Omens" and "Sometimes the Ache Sleeps"
New Delta Review, "At the Construction Site"
PP/FF: An Anthology, "Moonflower"
paragraph, "Almost Enough"
Pearl, "Again"
Poetry East, "Like Stars"
Puerto del Sol, "Day Beginning with Rain"
Rhino, "Babies" and "Expectations"
Salamander, "Long White Hallway"
Sentence, "Almost Sweet" and "Still Reticent"
Sudden Stories: A Mammoth Anthology of Miniscule Fiction, "Joe" and "Pretty Heart"
Third Coast, "The Only Story Left" and "When Sorrow Arrives"
Willow Springs, "Broken Stove" and "Math"
The Rose Metal Press Field Guide to Prose Poetry, "Wish"

"Cure" was reprinted in *Beloved on Earth: 150 Poems of Grief and Gratitude* (Holy Cow! Press).

"River Eye" appeared in the exhibition "Second Sight/Insight II" at the Kalamazoo Institute of Arts.

Some of these poems previously appeared in the chapbook *October Again* (Burnside Review Press, 2012).

Some of these poems previously appeared in the chapbook *Mended* (Kattywompus Press, 2014).

Contents

III.

IV.

I

Babies

wiggle their fat fingers and blow spit bubbles at me in the grocery store. In Colorado, older ones barrel straight down slopes much too steep for me while their shiny helmets gleam. They have clear eyes and snotty noses. Maybe I am looking? Surely, they have always been here: one burps formula on my sleeve and I find it hours later, dry smell of vomit. Vicki's son—just days old—lies on my couch, balanced too near the edge? My cat will bite.

I am not round as a pear. I am not the pear tree, either. I have thought of myself as a willow, fixed but moving in the breeze.

Ideal is a cliché. I won't argue. I have no remarks about my childhood in the abstract, even though someone in a darkened auditorium waits. So I have to say something. *At the time of conception,* I begin, *the soul makes a reservation,* and someone else lobs a tomato. Of course, the garden's overripe, overrun, but I only planted the seeds a week ago. And the vegetables grew up misshapen and huge, sickly green and dirty purple. No way can I set up a little vegetable cart in the yard, white with a green-striped awning and a money box, run on the honor system.

Lament

The heroine doesn't know if she wants a child. What kind of story is this? The red sand drains in the hourglass while she cries for her aunt and her dog and the flat Kansas sky. It's possible she's not playing the starring role. Because what woman cares only for herself, wants no complications? A small thief, by nature she's a keeper. A miser, too tired at the end of the day to want company, she can't make dinner fast enough and, stunned, eats scraps from the saucepan. Anything unnecessary is a scourge. A bane, like knocking her kneecaps continually on stumps while she walks in the woods. Whenever she sleeps, no one wakes her. She dreams the music of her bones is the clatter of forks in a drawer. But she might want a new shape. Unattached, she feels only a little pleasure. A little relief? She can't call it loneliness and it's not strong enough for hunger. Just a constant *what if?*

Omens

So where were the birds? *Everyone knows a bird in the house is an omen of death.* And all that fall, when my parents died, the birds stayed right where they belonged. They didn't even fly into windows. Black swarms rose up, then swerved like schools of fish, and once by the overpass I saw a hawk hovering, practically motionless, gliding on hot exhaust. I wish I'd turned the car around.

A bat once swooped through the house, then flew upstairs. I tried to follow, scared, but never found it. Does that count?

Technically, two birds should have found their way inside. Shall I lodge a complaint because we had only a fat and stupid possum on the walkway, a dead mouse with its tail chewed off? Then the first killing frost took the moonflower vine overnight. Sinister, but my mother was expecting it, as she wrote to a friend, she just couldn't say when.

Expectations

Await is more elegant, more terrifying than *wait*: the maiden awaits her fate. And if the jewel, if the admirer, never arrives? If her dress grows tighter by the day? The day falls down around the wish, still kicking.

It's natural to want to know what happens next: a phone call, a doctor's appointment? Vitamins? She doesn't know what could go wrong. The car could leave tire tracks on her white dress. The dog could beg and then roll over dead. For play. For the baby's sake.

Telling is more fun than waiting. But she has no one to tell. So she waits. First in the backyard, then in the house. She shows the guest to the room she has prepared. She says, *I thought you might come*. But his misgivings, his complaints arrive in an envelope slipped under her door. He has money; look what he doesn't want. The coins spill and clank on the dank basement floor. She never thought to listen down there.

More Expectations

Everyone said, *Save*, so we did and then we had a stone, a pebble at the bottom of the well. Which would not get hauled up or led on a leash, finding no rabbit, just scent. Maybe scent of cat next to dirty gutter water. A trickle, really. We'd picnicked near a field, not golden and alive in the wind, but plowed and not yet planted, not opportunity, just work, hard work and the unelegant sun.

Everyone saved, everyone waited, everyone sang their whispered song behind my back and unsure, I wouldn't answer. Or I hedged my bets, answered in fragments. Everyone called above the children's voices, made jokes with real questions behind them: *see what you're missing?*

I got dizzy in the library when I read the titles on the top shelf. I told one person, one only: the man in the waiting room who offered chocolates each time he wanted one himself. So that was twice, two crinkly gold wrappers I folded and unfolded while I watched the sky outside, a gray expanse of concrete I could roller-skate across, or cartwheel, being careful not to skin my knees.

Joe

We take the boy with one leg out in our boat. That he has one leg is not his fault: no accident or lapse, just bad luck. He throws his crutches in the truck, hops, then grabs his friend's baseball cap. I've met him twice. Today's his grace. He balances on one ski around the lake, around the only other boat, a family fishing, who nearly drop their poles and stare: a one-legged boy, did you see that? A contraption held up with ropes and mirrors, speed and light. Seen from another angle, it's the same imperfect picture: he grins. He's playing. I don't ask, *Do you think about dying?* How stupid of me, how gloom and doom. He watches for girls in bikinis. We're all dying. That's one way of thinking: the foghorn's deep groan can't rescue us, lost in our boats. But in the noon sun of Saturday, he's blonde and tan and lanky, the picture of sixteen, so far from how he began: a tiny package, rosy and sleepy, ten fingers, ten toes.

Math

Must I answer every mouth? I want a little quiet water, a patch of midmorning sun, but are my flimsy desires just math? I am good at addition but this is not simple. The letters follow, a steady stream, adding themselves to the pile on the hearth. I will not let you open one, but here is the problem: how to divide, divide again, and then not end up clichéd, wearing a housecoat. Subtle: if you add, must you subtract? One and one make one, part of both, who then can never rest again: to the relatives it is something to giggle about. Because they've also been up all night with a cranky baby? Two children in a red wagon are heavier to pull than you'd think, even for a short distance. Enter the season of disgust, the carpet chosen to hide dirt, the leaky ceiling nearly collapsing. Do I believe the mother who said her baby never cried? Look what she gave up—some part—but doesn't the part return, multiplied? In the clamor, the football thrown against the walls, the pairs and pairs of muddy shoes, does anyone notice?

Shallow

The moon has no mouth, never nibbled at my walls, never nested in sunflower seeds or yellow insulation. Poker-faced and rocky, why should she care about me? A certain pink, missing. The cheek not warm or innocent. Her light through our bedroom window washes color from us: the problem lies inadequate in that silky glow. No fool, the moon's never wanted a mouth stained with strawberries or one wiped clean. Nothing as noisy or elaborate as a dug-up iris forgotten on the lawn, roots attached. She is pinned to the sky, unapproachable: to be aloof, to be cold and disinterested and not afraid if anyone knows is a decent strategy. She can look mournful or playful, depending on mood, and even then it's pure interpretation. Yours. Her own plate-face shines in every pill, shallow. A cobweb tangles in your eyelash; the silken thread sticks and sticks, insistent before the holiday parade, insistent before the picnic with my potato salad, suddenly gluey: it wasn't good and the guests didn't lie nicely, didn't lie at all. I, the cook, took my cues from the moon in her gummy light, fading and glowing. Liars with pledges of love have taken advantage of her, she is sure, but she, level-headed, is unforgiving and precise as a clock. Hollow and bald as a gumball. Accused of everything.

The Accident

In twilight, they made a pact. The father and the mother who didn't have a child. Then they ate clams. They went to live among scrub and dust and cactus. The woman who was not a mother put her hands inside coyotes: she cut their stomachs open to see what they ate. He swam and she ran. Could such happiness last? For years, they lived like that but now he measures it in days. Red dust from the road gathered in her kitchen's corners while she dreamed of ropes and coyotes. In her dream, one friend asked, *Are you ever having kids?* She planted seeds, took notes on coyotes, and then a baby came. She thought her life was hers. That was the joke. *Sorry, sorry,* called the crows. But the crows pleased the baby, eight months old, who shook her rattle at them. So nothing could be done. *Nothing could have been done,* the doctor said, softly, when the mother was found by the side of the road.

The father said, *This is a family matter.* But the reporters came. The police sought the driver. The father said, *I'll always hate twilight,* though the accident happened in morning's bright light. Black and chattering, the crows called out his sorrow. Her absence was so large it emptied him and the faded landscape the sun moved across, over and over.

Wish

I demanded, when available, five to eight theories of sleep, including the whereabouts of our dreamselves during waking hours: twice in the night I've fallen for the touch that lingered, the luscious kiss on my bare shoulder. I couldn't help dreaming it. Such a pretty story: in love like stuck in mud. The weather inside my head got better when couples sat on green park benches in the rose garden. But the names were wrong. They didn't know a rose was no talisman. My wish was short—a blue mitten no larger than a thumb, no larger than a dime, a wish so small. And it rose into the air.

Still Reticent

May I say I have a secret? Over days, tiny stars bloomed on feathery stems in the field. They had begun as small green knobs. Of course I mean daisies, but may I say this? Mother, may I? I look the same. I act the same. But am I changed? A clock ticks in a small bare room, lit with soft peach light. Some days, the clock looks like an egg. Some days, a pearl. The room is my secret: it is not inside any house. Whether the room is filled with calm is a matter of opinion: the clock grows a pendulum and a square glass face, grows too large to stand up straight, so the pendulum flops like a dying fish; it curls like a comma, like a pink shrimp.

You will not find the door to this room in the same place twice.

Like Stars

I am walking when a small patch of overcast sky clears. It is almost evening, and the sun shines on white birds against darker sky. Just then, the insects stop buzzing and their silence feels like presence. The birds reflect the light like stars. Huge bright flocks move their weight across the sky. Right now my friend is having a baby boy who is expected to die.

River Eye

I crouched by the river and scooped Death into my palm. He'd fledged too soon but had not struggled long. A triangle of shadow pooled around us. He turned away while he panted and tried to work his wet wings. Like a cathedral, the bridge arched its sturdy elegance over us. Light loved that emptiness so much it could hardly bear to leave.

Death cocked a glassy eye at me, reflected sleek water, feathery leaves, chain link around the day's last light. A line of concrete columns, diminishing. Death opened wide and I fed him live crickets for his long journey. Above us, sky kept right on vanishing.

Two Kinds of Anger

A possum on the dirt road, pink mouth open, insides bare to sky. Alive with flies. Their mechanical buzz rises into the day, into the promise of heat shimmering over the swamp. A swallowtail, its yellow wings bright with sun, dips and swoops through the swarm. It lands at the wound to feed.

II

Details

After Easter dinner, my nephew asks, *What's a detail?* and my mother replies, *It's a part of the story.* He accepts this answer. We are reading; rude Squirrel Nutkin has just been captured by Great Brown Owl when my father falls down by the dining room table. I try to read in just the same voice as before so my nephew won't be scared, even though I am. But I don't hate my father for something he can't help, I hate the falling. I hate the outward appearance of weakness. My brother is holding my father's arm. I've never asked him what he thinks of Dad's frailty. Squirrel Nutkin escapes without being eaten but doesn't change his impertinent ways: he still won't offer the owl minnows or berries or nuts. That's part of the story. Another part of a different story: my mother looked up and saw my father at the end of the dock with the dog. Mist began to gather over the lake and the railing wasn't yet installed. The rain had trampled the daffodils during this, the season of rebirth. Later, my brother untangled a set of car keys from the ivy at the water's edge. My mother thanked him profusely for such small things, such details: for finding the keys, for raising my father up.

Everlasting

Wasps climb into my windows; bats crawl under the eaves. The crickets, too many to count, don't stop chirping when I enter the basement. Some things I chose: the house, specifically, and the other person in it. The view came with the house. The cat came from my mother-in-law.

But a seed for a yellow sunflower came in the packet by mistake. I liked it best: it cheered me up, and now it is gone. Even I hardly noticed, at first, how my father's hand trembled, how slowly he turned his head. His idea of heaven is knowing where everything he lost went. Not getting it back. Just knowing. I notice people notice him, and then notice something's not right. Because he can't say *hello* clearly, or stand up straight and balanced with somewhere to put his hands.

This September light fools my morning glories and they bloom well into afternoon. The blue are more everlasting than the pink, though even that word fools itself. A candy, also everlasting, lived up to its name in a book I loved as a child. But the story is never the same from this distance, now when I can't help but see the flaws.

Disease, in the Particular

I floated rose-petal boats across the ocean. Forgive me that romance, that dopey soap-opera gesture. At least the roses were not red. And waterlogged, they did not travel far. Did they reach my father near the ocean, not without hope? So why not say, full of hope, the most hopeful man I know? His brain disease is real, stark and incurable, so slow, so nearly imperceptible its progression, so—can I say this?—gentle, and so gentle his decline, how can I not cry? I cannot hope to lift him out of his stiffening limbs and set him down shiny and baptized into the rest of his life. Look what fun we would have had! I have some money, mostly thanks to him. But money cannot help. So I can say easily, saintly: yes. Yes, take it all, take everything, every last dime.

Joy

The sky fills with wings that erase the Christmas card in my hand: *We hope this year brought you as much joy as the birth of our children brought us.* Here's my own pale gesture, pale reply: the corn finally grew and the barn swallows returned. My hothouse tulips, purple and delivered in January, closed their delicate eyes for five nights before they died. I left a green apple in the snow and a raccoon joyfully dragged it away. A squirrel hurled itself against my window twice. My joy, small and untended, eclipsed nothing. The radio said, out of context, *Suffering is a privilege.* My best joy is sleep, which leads to the moment just before waking. I open and open my eyes: birds rush upward, wings brushing my cheeks like tears.

Fallen

This maple leaf, fallen, is leathery like a turtle's shell, delicately arched and ridged. Color of sunset, color of flame, it requires no explanations. Too pretty to look immortal, it does not speak. It does not ask what will become of it. But I am greedy and mean. I think terrible thoughts about friends and like my dog better than most people I meet. I want money and dream of getting some, but am too lazy to go to real work each day, progress that can be measured by number. I want the best things for myself: the larger slice of cake, the pink quartz rock I've found to keep in my pocket. Above all, I want sleep but sleep on my side, turned away from what I love.

When Sorrow Arrives

You will not want to believe this. You must let her in, no matter what she smells of—burning leaves and Murphy's Oil Soap, our mother's lavender sachets. Offer her your softest pillow, clean sheets, leek soup. She didn't break your heart.

She likes lilies, how their creamy trumpets perfume the air. When the lilies and their rich scent vanish, she's still here, playing football with the neighborhood kids. Her touch marks them with an ache like a grass stain. Do not warn them against her, even when she leads them to a small brown snake sunning itself by the lake. Even when she does not stop them from killing it with sticks and rocks.

Again

Never conceived, never arrived into the light and the clatter and the chill. Never rapt, like a statue. Never arrived for the slap, bright hurt to greet the world. Indelible, pearly, my grief's stain: luminous and fragile and grim. We'd thought a lucky quilt might help, instead of science's imprecise answer. It seemed a stubborn, stupid kind of hope in face of the facts, and even the facts were speechless. So he didn't bring germs home, he carefully changed his clothes. Perform, I asked my body. I asked my body to behave predictably just once, like clockwork, though a bronze clock, watchful, says precision is its own sorrow. The clock has a man's face—maybe the man in the moon, indifferent and diseased. Or Diana? Its bronze cheeks draw up in a smile, apple-witty. You will have heard this before: a solid weight, shriveled; that bright balloon, possibility, then nothing.

Almost Enough

The lake is smooth and brooding. Turtles climb out. I press my nose to the window and the sparrow in my heart lifts its wings. No sun today, but still the air is bright with light from the lake. I didn't want to mention love, but this morning the lake shone gold and maroon and the cat and dog climbed on the bed with me. The falling leaves blew through our yard. And four swans drifted into view. I raised my head and they were there, unsummoned, a gift. I will admit this season makes me cold enough to think four white swans are a sign, my heart floating in fresh water. But swans separate themselves from loss as they bend their necks under water. Yesterday, I walked through a red sunset to mail letters. From here, I can see the dog's heart beating in her chest. The swans are still floating, although I know they're not weightless, and do not see me.

Waiting

I ask you this in confidence: is my time running out? Don't tell me Vicki's baby blankets look cheap, because such a word, such a turn of phrase never applied to her. Do you want to argue? Shall we come to blows? *I've had it up to here!* my mother would shout, then chase us up the stairs with a wooden spoon. The gentle taps and pats on our backs didn't leave marks. What do such actions suggest? What does the play say about the nature of love? Start with wings: why struggle under their weight? The summer we backpacked in Europe, we bought the lightest souvenirs we could find—three ceramic egg cups, because we figured we'd break one. And though we haven't yet, I've been wrong before. Look how I kept everyone waiting—the news this month is bad again. Twice, recently, two women exclaimed, *You look so young!* Privately, they mean, younger than themselves. . . . The crowd stamped their feet and blew on their hands, tired of bad news. True, they gathered without my consent, wanting to swaddle and cuddle. Believe me, I understand the prospect of comfort. Its allure. Its shining appeal.

Notes on 'The Accident'

I knew you had dogs—I didn't know their names—and they were jealous of your baby. I never met your husband or saw your house in Arizona. I knew you hated to lose things, but had to buy another plane ticket to Chicago, another college algebra book. I keep dreaming I've misplaced my baby—did you?

Years ago, at Wendy's wedding, you wanted to be married; your eyes filled but the tears didn't spill over. I didn't touch you because I thought a touch would make you cry more. Then you said, *I believe Jesus died for me.*

I know you remember this: the summer after we graduated, we met in Detroit, in front of the Renaissance Center's fountain. You arrived first: tall, lanky, short brown hair, and smiling broadly. The fountain's rainbows glistened behind you. The last time I saw you, I told you I always thought of you in this moment, walking towards me and smiling.

Broken Stove

He tried to liken breaking the stove to throwing money out the window, but it wasn't quite that—the stove slid, then lifted by wind, flipped from the truck: glittery crash, splash of glass. And Lady Luck, who'd neglected us, shrugged, so at least the stove landed on no one. A mistake's a mistake: simple to have tied it down. Careless, he'd ruined an expensive gift. He hated for them to think it, hated being left behind while money rose into the air. We agreed we'd say *We hadn't thought a stove could fly* if the stove's giver asked, which was a kind of truth. But we had to have one—we'd given our old one away—so we talked and drove, talked and drove, while babysitting a child of five, who said all that talk made him tired. So tired he laid down on the appliance store's floor in his blue coat, then inched slowly across, a small boat on a shiny ocean of stoves.

My Anger

Today I sent My Anger to yoga at 5 a.m. I set out her water bottle and mat, which she dropped, along with the car keys, after she closed the door. When she came home, she slammed the dishwasher and threw bruised apples and stale chips in our lunch bags. Then My Anger posted another complicated chore chart with a row of black check marks after her name.

She has always lived with me. Often when I wake, she's cleaning the basement. I bring her coffee, milk, and a chocolate bar on my grandmother's wooden tray. My Anger shows me the boxes where she files her spreadsheets. When we sit together on the cool floor, when I admire the work she's done, anyone would think we were friends. I wish My Anger would linger on the screen porch and watch the hummingbirds' throats. She has called me to the window only once, when a hawk flew low across our field gripping a small brown bird, a bird it will eat.

Siege

Not inside the fence or house, please, I shout. *You know the rules.* These children never listen. They refuse to leave. Covered in frost, even the trees seem more delicate, more breakable and fleeting. Barefoot and greedy, these children want everything that glitters. One child climbs the ladder to the power line, to the tippy top, then dives over the fence into the ferns, soft as feathers. The catalpa flowers are stiff as starched lace. A huge flock of birds circles and lands, circles and swoops. One blue bird is at the feeder, the rest are all black. They darken the sky. Another child lands flat on his back, bounces, then somersaults to his feet, just fine. I'm a loud voice in the plumage: I yell and no one listens, I use my outside voice. I don't get as far as goodbye. Their bad black dog digs up my morning glories. I can't fix everything myself. Upstairs, my husband shouts, *Children in the house!* But how? Some hide in the bushes or behind the lampposts that have sprouted in the yard. Others ring the doorbell at dinner time and stay to watch us eat.

Proposal

The skinny young man had a plan: he needed me to live with him and his (wife? lover? friend?) because they couldn't have a child, which I would provide. The woman (love of his life?) stood slightly apart while he explained. He wasn't mournful but lived under her exacting eye. She didn't speak. She was calm. But a little girl followed him, a little girl old enough to run and jump, old enough to have hair down to her shoulders. Wasn't she the child he sought? My presence was necessary, he explained, as in the case of the woman in the wheelchair. I had not read the papers because my subscription was cut off. I shouted: *I'm a terrible risk.* Shameful, sordid: wanted for the wrong reasons was worse than not being wanted at all. Our home, one room, would be done soon and we would need to warm it. But I walked on the bricklayers' hands while they set the bricks in cement. Or was it mortar, the gluey gray glop? My feet were stuck. The girl chased a flame-colored bird. He touched my arm and the touch felt real, solid despite its flaws. Why couldn't I be practical?

No Comfort

My watch, small mechanical heart, counts each tick, each minute lost from sleep. It's no comfort, though it should be; its round, benevolent face glows. It's no comfort adding seconds to what I've already lost: my good sense, my level head, grandmother's diamond ring. I could raise my voice and every object, all my earthly clutter, would listen. My heart's small mutterings are not monsoons, not tidal waves. I've thought about a man in a black leather jacket all day. More than is good for me. And thinking's only half: after I hear the possum eating garbage in the garage, I plan to kill it. It's no comfort knowing the killing gets easier each time. Don't tell me it's possibility, that graceless and insatiable animal, without sense enough to hide from its hunger.

III

Another Ache

I thought I ached because of something I ate. None of my clothes fit though I tried them all and left piles of velvet and denim on the floor. A black spider, large as a brooch, larger than the one I floated down the drain, crept over my earrings on the dresser. See what I am capable of?

Do you want to hear it all? First, I want the rumbling in the floor to stop. I said that a bird—a large one—doesn't fly into the car window because someone wished it. I said the relatives never sent thank-you notes for our gifts.

Then the suitcase fell off and the tire exploded. Then the driver got out to look at the lake, its calm expanse. We all felt worse because nothing had been predicted, no sign of trouble on such a sunny day—road salt glittered its million cheap promises, strands of videotape flashed brown, then bright, in that clean light.

Pretty Heart

Pretty heart, my doctor says, looking at the ultrasound monitor. I want to know: *Is it whole?* I'm alarmed by what science has told me precisely: the baby's weight and sex and brain size . . . and statistical chances of terrible defects. Today we see his tongue move, inside his mouth, inside me, his own small ocean. Cross-sectioned (*like if you cut a salami in half,* the sonographer explains), the heart's four small dark circles, marbles, miniature moons, bluebird eggs—that fragile?—the flutters quick, irregular. I recognize it when they point it out: pretty. I hope she means it's formed the way it should. I don't want to hear about heads or hearts that don't grow, or grow wrong, instead of this pretty one we've got. Suddenly, I can't say it, can't ask, *What if?* Can't ask—*those babies—their hearts— The initial test results,* my doctor says, *don't change.* I can't think. Instead I'm seeing wallpaper, blue blankets, blue moons, weighing luck and science, in unequal doses, with our baby's new socks, arranged in his dresser for months, waiting in darkness, small and secret, like he is, like we are.

Birth Poem

Mention mother and I think of birth—my son's, five months ago—and blood and cramps and more people putting their hands inside me than I can stand. Someone drew four vials of blood and left quarter-sized bruises on my arm. Dizzy, I watched the blood, thick and dark. Urine, feces, amniotic fluid—they tested it all. The vomit they disposed of. They carefully measured what went in and what came out. No matter—everything forced itself out. *I feel so strange*, I said. But it felt good to hold handfuls of ice and sleep on wet sheets though I couldn't swallow the glass of ice water I'd dreamed about. My room had no lock, but my favorite nurses knocked. People said later, *You poor thing! Nine weeks flat on your back.* No one said, *If you get up, your baby will die.* The nurses all said, *This will give you something to write about.*

Writing's more private than birth. No poem's lifted out whole, like my son. But some, like him, in need. And—with luck—a moment of grace . . . A stranger, a doctor, held my hand while another stitched me up.

Long White Hallway

I wait for you there, pushing the baby in his stroller. The baby claps his hands with concentration and delight. A tiny, black-haired woman's cut cheek bleeds as I walk from Emergency to Intensive Care and back again. She presses a Kleenex to her face and wipes away blood. We are helpless when our bodies fail—is that why I can't turn away? I wonder at what distance I'll recognize your face and voice. And wonder—after we die, will we find each other?

Here, we wait for news. I eat animal crackers from a vending machine because my mother's bone scan takes longer than it should. Finally, a woman in a white coat asks if I need directions, *Because*, she says, *you've been walking for so long. Just waiting*, I say. *Just waiting* sounds like *just looking*, as if I've entered an elegant store where I can't afford anything and can't wait to leave.

My Anger at Home

Occasionally, on mild and sunny afternoons, My Anger will take a book and a blanket and walk so far into our field I can't see her anymore. Blue jays quarrel in the oaks while a rhythmic insect buzz surrounds the house. A cricket calls from the hot garage. I almost forget My Anger out there in all that green. When she comes back, flushed and quiet, she shakes out her blanket and asks me to check her for ticks. She is so polite, so small and pliable then, it is easy to do what she asks. The smell of lilacs rises up as I brush her hair. She might let me kiss her, lightly. She might let me pull the sheet up to her chin.

Sometimes the Ache Sleeps

When my dad reached unsteadily from his wheelchair to put my baby's sock back on, the baby clapped and waved. When I helped my mom to the bathroom, she whispered, *My little girl.* By then the ache was all around us. But each day the purple morning glories bloomed after the sun rose, and each day promised to be just like the one before. On a scrap of yellow paper, my mother wrote *Never give up,* and taped it to the mirror.

Stay

When I set up the cot in her room, my mother says, *You must sleep upstairs with your husband.* But when the baby wakes, I nurse him upstairs while my husband stays with her.

I'll never know which part of exhaustion came from grief. The baby opens his bedroom door at night and calls me. When I appear, he is delighted. He kisses me, jams his forehead against my cheek, then pulls back suddenly, to get a good look at me.

Flight

When I put my palm on my mother's chest, I feel her heartbeat. Then it stops. The nurse is in our family room, zooming you around like an airplane. Sometimes you laugh. Sometimes you reach for her dark hair.

After

I hadn't expected to like the undertaker, a man young as my brother who arrived at the house within an hour, who told us his mother died the week before. I'd expected his firm handshake, his dark suit. But he said, *I've come at a bad time,* because I had raised one finger—*wait a minute, please*—before I opened the door, so I could complain about the hospice nurse who said, over and over, my mother had *expired* (like milk, like a parking meter).

Two men were needed to lift my mother from the bed, even though she was small; I liked how the second man stayed outside until then. When I gave him a gray blanket with satin trim, the young undertaker said, *That's nice and soft.* He had brought a green one, softer than it looked. When I asked, he uncovered my mother's face and let me arrange the blanket. If we wished, we could still see her in the morning. Then we walked outside, the undertakers with the stretcher, me and my brother behind. We approached the hearse's open back door, the men didn't slow, and I thought, crazily, expecting a crash, *I should have helped lift it,* but the stretcher clicked, then kneeled, then slid right in and then they shut the door.

After II

After the undertaker took my mother, after the hospice nurse left,
I peeked at her pink flowered comforter (had the undertaker made
the bed?), her red glass lamp, her tiny porcelain birds, each feather
on each wing accurate. Everything was still hers—even the crumpled
Kleenex and Vaseline, the eyedropper for ice water, the bottle of
liquid morphine—and my cot was still next to her bed. I turned on
the light, went in, inhaled. *What if she's come back?* Just as fast, I was
ashamed—I just wanted to see her again.

Punishment

I'd like my pain removed. Set aside, in an old tin can. I'd have surgery. I'd give birth. I'd shit it out and have a look. I doubt my body has turned it to pearl. It must be a web, a glistening tangle. Like a wet butterfly net, a lump of fishing line. Insubstantial. Nearly weightless, smelling of stagnant swamp water, something dead beside the road. Sorrow thinks I've got it wrong, begs me to reconsider. I don't care. I'd set the can in my backyard, on a hot, hot day. When it's good and rotten, maybe a possum will eat it. Until then, let it sit and think about what it's done.

Morning

The morning after my mom's memorial, I dreamed I told her who came. *Mrs. Goetcheus, just back from visiting the Molotkeys in Arizona,* I said, and sipped my tea. From our bay window, the lake looked like it did every November, its surface a dull nickel, indistinguishable from gray sky; three ducks dove to the bottom, then popped back up again. *She said Don thought about coming, too.* My mother said, *That's nice,* not sick or frail as she swallowed her toast.

Then we were quiet, the same comfortable quiet of 4 a.m. when we both couldn't sleep—she from pain, me after the baby woke me. Nothing in the room held its breath—not my grandmother's china cabinet, dark and solid as always, a spray of beach grass in a vase on top; not the toy rocking horse nodding on the bookshelf. Until the clock engraved with my father's name stops. Then I want to ask, *What do you believe happens after you die?* but stop myself—because that is private. Because asking doesn't change anything. Because I am still scared of what she might say.

At Ten Months

At ten months old, what has my son learned about death? He has seen my mother's face every day for two months. He has waved to her across the table, shared his cracker, wiggled on his back across her floor. He knows he can summon me by making a fuss. But now, no matter what he does, he cannot call her into the room.

Almost Sweet

All day I check on the dove, dead on the deck, and wish, each time I look, it might rise up, though I heard it smack against glass, saw it drop, tremble, shake its injured wing, then lay its head down. It was gentle, almost sweet, that last gesture. And now, just after, I want to say, *We all end that way*, as if dying were as easy as falling asleep. But that's not right, either. After my mother lay down, she waited four days. I slept in her room, did what little I could—Vaseline for her lips, then a teaspoon of water. When would the gentleness come? Maybe the moment after. Or the moment after that.

Near the Angel

The angel's outline under last night's snow is almost invisible, the valleys of her wings and legs a shadowy X, low ridges the wind could have shaped. But it was not chance; you lay down to make her.

The silver garbage can, near the angel, near the birdfeeders, is new and neat and perfect, under its cold white cap. Its lid, shiny and undented, fits tightly. Today I am in love with this sturdy container, full of cold seeds. The snow does not look like anyone's ashes. When the sun shone, when I chased the baby away from the stove, my yard was too bright to look at for long.

Prayer for Disappearing

If only I could learn to become breath, to leave my body and settle in the house, a still and constant presence. While we sleep, lightning blinks through the aspen. Our flashlight is lost. Our son's tooth is lost. The skunk sidesteps our trap and noses up dirt around the foundation. Our breathing, unremarkable, goes on like always. Come morning, the sky will hold both sun and moon while four swallows dip and swoop through humid air.

IV

At the Construction Site

I fall from the roof of the new house. My mother, small below me,
opens her red mouth. I catch the startled balloons her words make.
Now, hawks and starlings circle me, giant fledgling gone wrong.
Their sharp claws and beaks are not terrible: they could bring me
my mother's voice once again.

My Anger Sleeps Over

Here she comes in her blue fleece jacket, her overnight bag stuffed with rhinestones and rocks, her teeth and hair brushed. When My Anger wants food she'll reject what you offer. Already she's upended her suitcase in your living room, already she's balanced her stuffed cormorant on your mantle, already snatched up a hammer and scared your tremulous cat. Where does the time go? Her shoelaces are knotted, her face scratched, and the bus she needs to catch is minutes away. Maybe you thought My Anger would never act this way in your home—you'd read her a poem about a swan or guide her to the bench near the peonies you've reserved for cloud-watching. Together you would breathe and count to ten. It's possible you did nothing to deserve this. It's possible My Anger might sit, take your hand, and tilt her face toward the sky.

Onion

Because its skin is on, this onion doesn't smell pungent. It is a hot air balloon, a baby's bald head with one unruly hair. Egg-size, egg-weight, it won't crack. The root end's rough like sandpaper. Or an eraser—to erase what?

This onion enters church in my pocket, and then just once a year. Its smell is invisible, like God. Pure white, its fragile skin makes me blink. How does God's glory smell? Are wings made of the same glimmery skin? Will I see glory in my refrigerator, and will it make me cry?

I want to be forgiven for lying to my mother about how her stove broke, for ignoring the neighbor girls whose mother swears at them, and for wanting—just once—my father to die quickly and unexpectedly, instead of bit by bit, every day, every month, with me here watching.

The Only Story Left

Their parents left them, a boy and a girl, brother and sister, in the vast wild world of raspberry brambles and dogwood, lawyers and fast-talking brokers. Brokenhearted, sick, heartsick. Full up with grief. The mother said, *Be brave.* The father said, *I'll see you tomorrow.* Then they died.

And some people watched and some people helped and some people sighed and said, *They couldn't live without each other.*

The lake said nothing and the girl loved its promise not to ease her grief. The gray Cape Cod house said nothing. And the possum under the porch kept gnawing into it. Because the house was full of food and love? Or because the possum had teeth and had to use them for something?

Sorrow Came

Because she was called. Like the minister, like the undertaker, she speaks softly. When no one else will, she mentions my parents. How my mother loved butterscotch. How my father loved socket sets.

Now I am used to her. She spends all day looking at the back of my head. If I turn, she turns too.

When I learn everything about her, will she go?

Grief's Pretty Prize

Today I am all mouth, unsatisfied. The dictionary won't say how to erase the ache. What have I filled by the end of the day? Glasses of water, bushels of peaches. Given a recipe, everyone expects clarity, expects of the three wishes, one will be for perfect pie crust, which vanishes, as it should, into a family's mouths. They have gathered around a table. I know I shouldn't say they are bathed in light. But look—

a whole family, not one member gone. The mouth in the sky or the earth has closed, temporarily full: grief has not begun with them. But I am grief's pretty prize. For now, imagine me in the hospital's hallways, lit by green exit signs, pushing the baby's stroller longer than you'd think I could, in that clean bright light, away from someone I love.

My Anger Takes a Road Trip

Right now My Anger's stuck on a two-lane highway under construction, slowly driving past heaps of concrete and bent rebar, a pile of burning tires sending up tarry smoke. She likes how the long grass in the median bows down as she goes by. Near the overpass, a bunny the size of her hand crouches in the weeds. My Anger sets it on the concrete, stirs the flames, and reaches for a sandhill crane made of steel, each outstretched feather a razor. She wants to flatten the lindens shading the riverwalk, their delicate perfumed bells opening over her head. She wants to uproot the tin sunflowers that line County Road 81. Next to the highway, cattle lie in dirt stockyards that stretch for miles. My Anger likes to imagine she is one of the last to see those animals alive.

Day Beginning with Rain

No one looks for me in the shadows of the lake or the day. A man rises out of the water, pushing a large deer toward shore. I can see its ribs and somehow it is alive and bends its neck to me. The man goes back into the water. We can absorb any wing, even single ones, and still this counts as flight. What we expect: the page to fall away and leave us standing near the boat in the rain, the wind shaking the trees with a self-imposed impatience, inertia. Well, then, why not change more than the color of your hair, the music of the wind? Whenever you want, touch the mirror, touch the sore tooth simply to feel the pain, a quick torch like a kiss. The sun sinking in the sky, earlier and earlier, like desire and its sudden absence, even this makes me nervous. It is possible to move through the days without the moon, without a clear image of what one loves best in the world. The dog licks the pages of the book and watches the rain. What can we do but change our style of weeping? I am tired of looking for myself, tired of testing the shock I could withstand. Melancholy is not as bad as sadness, is not the heart's worst color. Though there are things blacker than night: oil, for instance, and the smell of tar, and any horse's eyes.

Moonflower

After the first killing frost, the moonflower vine wilted, then rotted, on the white wood fence by my parents' front door. Inside the house, my mother was dying too. In the hospital, after her operation, she said, *I thought we'd have more time.* Then she told me to check the pockets of her dress clothes for money before I gave them away.

The vine smelled dead—an odd bad vegetable smell, leaves gone wet and translucent overnight. The smell grew worse every day. I thought the vine couldn't predict my mother's death. Nobody had promised the vine anything more than one summer to grow lush under my mother's care, to unfurl its plate-sized blossoms into the night. Nobody had promised it company either, but a purple morning glory sprouted; the vines tangled together. Like a mother and daughter? Nobody had promised it would be loved, or that my father would look upon it morning after morning before its blossoms closed.

Grief II

Is it melodramatic to say, *You wanted me?* Went to such lengths to get me, you must have eyed me from the start? Now I have a broken place in my chest that gets broken again, then not quite fixed, over and over and over. Another foreign mouth that does not speak.

On a lake empty of swans, on a calm lake in November, you break the surface, have always just stepped out of the room with my mother to fetch a shovel, to plant a dogwood or divide the daylilies. You break any surface— when the Medicare rep phones my mother to get my father's wheelchair back, I say, *My mother died too*, and, suddenly polite, she gives me a break.

You must have sent that fat and stupid possum to live under my parents' porch and scout things out, to eat garbage near the Chinese dogwood and waddle down the walk that night when I stood at the glass front door. The next morning I found a frozen mouse there, tail eaten, and swept it away so my mother wouldn't see your calling card, a warning I didn't want to read.

Seaside Lullaby for My Friend

Whisper your troubles into a shell's glossy ear. I'm on the other side. You're an island, I'm the palm waiting to be your boat. Find the way out. Next, I'll be your ocean. After you drop it, the seashell drifts to the sandy bottom, its ear sealed. Down here, no one cares what you make for dinner. We can swim in and out of shipwrecks all day if you want. But bedtime always comes. The sheets are pale and cool and ripple. Here's your drink of water. Close your eyes. Soon the glassy surface will reflect the dawn.

Letter to My Future Self

What is it like, having some of the answers? Do I feel any more self-assured? You're the only one who understands me, really. Plus you've got perspective. So tell me that the mortgage, the Valentine cupcakes for the first grade, the cat's ashes will fade quicker than I can imagine. Quicker, even, than I'd want. Every moment vanishes, even my daughter's fingers in my hair, our heads on the same pillow. When I move to get up, she takes her thumb out of her mouth and says sleepily, *You can lay your head down.*

I used to wonder if I'd amount to anything. But I am tired of that question now. I try to foil greed with generosity, evil with love. That sort of thing. It's not original but it's all I can think of. So, how am I doing? Any progress yet?

Lament at Bath Time

Again, you fill the blue cup and drink, chew your toothbrush. You empty your cup on your head, then gasp and blink. I sing about the sea and a submarine. You hold your cup to our gray cat's mouth; he watches from tub's edge. After I lift you, dripping, to your white towel, you lean your whole just-washed self into my chest. And then stay.

Even this cannot erase my grief. Oh, Charlie, how can I bear it? Someday you'll feel this ache.

Cure

Take the red sailboat out; plant the garden. Every summer, I do something for the first time without my parents. Every summer, I wash my mother's hair, comb my father's, help them into clean pajamas . . .

And after, a bird lands in my hand to eat seeds, then pauses
above me for the white feather in my fingers

and grief lifts a little, the bird bears it up,
swallow or chickadee or wren,
and leaves a space . . .

my father's exhaled breath, my mother's reflection, before the stone, before she went away . . .

Prayer Inside Your Sleep

Let me build a shelter inside your sleep, tunnel, fort or hole large enough for my pillow and chair; let your sleep drift around me and carry me back from the numbered future; let your sleep cradle me through starless hours until dawn; let your sleep efface me; let your sleep offer a nest, a leaf, a tree I might inhabit, logic unspooling like the thread a spider pays out to escape—

Let the tide of your sleep rise again and again, perfected. Let your sleep dream of its own perfection. Let the field of your sleep ripple and bow under my breath, unperturbed as sky. Let your sleep flicker behind my eyelids. Let the cricket of your sleep creak softly, like a closing door.

Here, Where I Am, in October

Trees offer their stained glass leaves to the light. Wind ripples the lake and carries the fallen ones to shore. Clouds thin as smoke rise up. You know how beautiful all this is. There, wherever you are, do you have weather? This question no longer absorbs me. My grief is barely a shadow now. A brown snake, sunning itself on the dirt road, does not move when I walk by. A woodpecker taps, insistent. This world is not a mirror, with each of us on opposite sides. Here, where I am, a hunter has dumped the halves of a skinned deer and left its head resting on its tangled legs. The flies have not found it yet. A cricket chirps the same note again and again. The sun warms me. The wind moves through the trees like breath.

A Note from the Author

Thank you to my family and friends for everything.

"Like Stars" is for Mimi, Andrew and Benjamin Rassi.
"Notes on 'The Accident'" is for Martha Camp.

I am deeply grateful, over and over, to Tom Lombardo for selecting and believing in my poems, working with me to rearrange this book, and his careful to attention to my poems over multiple, thorough readings. Thank you to Jack Ridl, my first teacher, who is still teaching me twenty-seven years later. Thank you to the members of my writing groups, both in person and online, for their insight and advice, and for making my writing life a little less lonely. I am especially grateful to Nin Andrews, Sharon Bryan, Cullen Bailey Burns, Rick Bursky, Margaret DeRitter, Sammy Greenspan, Shivani Mehta, Yvonne Murphy, Karen Schubert, and Julie Stotz-Ghosh. And to my loves, Rhys, Charlie, and Lucy: infinite gratitude.

Kathleen McGookey's prose poems and translations have appeared in many journals and anthologies, including *Crazyhorse*, *Denver Quarterly*, *Epoch*, *Field*, *Ploughshares*, *Prairie Schooner*, *Quarterly West*, *The Best of The Prose Poem: An International Journal*, *The Party Train: A Collection of North American Prose Poetry*, and *The House of Your Dream: An International Collection of Prose Poetry*. The forthcoming anthology *Nothing to Declare: A Guide to the Flash Sequence* includes her work, and her poetry collection, *At the Zoo*, will be published by White Pine Press in spring 2017. She has received grants from the Irving S. Gilmore Foundation, the Arts Fund of Kalamazoo County, the Sustainable Arts Foundation, and the French Ministry of Foreign Affairs. She has taught creative writing at Hope College, Interlochen Arts Academy, and Western Michigan University. She lives in Middleville, Michigan, with her family.

Cover artist Dawn D. Surratt studied art at the University of North Carolina at Greensboro as a recipient of the Spencer Love Scholarship in Fine Art. She has exhibited her work throughout the Southeast and currently works as a freelance designer and artist. Her work has been published internationally in magazines, on book covers, and in print media. She lives on the beautiful Kerr Lake in northern North Carolina with her husband, one demanding cat and a crazy Pembroke Welsh Corgi.

Lightning Source UK Ltd.
Milton Keynes UK
UKOW03f0113040117
291285UK00002B/270/P